# BIG CATS

SCHOLASTIC

Library of Congress Cataloging-in-Publication Data

Evans, Lynette.
  Big cats / by Lynette Evans.

ISBN 13: 978-0-545-13894-9
ISBN 10: 0-545-13894-9

A CIP catalog record for this book is available from the Library of Congress.

Published in the United States by
**Scholastic Inc.**
557 Broadway
New York, New York 10012
www.scholastic.com

SCHOLASTIC and associated logos are trademarks and/or registered trademarks of Scholastic Inc.

16  17  18  19  20  21  22
18  17  16  15  14  13  12  11  10  9

Printed in China through Colorcraft Ltd., Hong Kong

**Author:** Lynette Evans
**Designer:** Matthew Alexander
**Photo Researcher:** Jamshed Mistry

**Photographs by: Big Stock Photo:** ©Daniel Leon (lioness, p. 6); ©Petr Masek (p. 25); **Corel** (tiger, p. 3); **Getty Images** (pp. 16–17; lion, cheetah, pp. 22–23); **Ingram Image Library** (lion, p. 3); **iStockphoto. com:** ©Eric Isselee (cat, p. 3); ©Kristian Sekulic (lion, p. 11); ©Robert Rushton (hyena, p. 11); **Photodisc** (tiger, p. 7); **Photolibrary** (landscape, background, pp. 2–3; cheetah cubs, p. 3; cheetah, p. 6; pp. 8–9; cheetah and cubs, pp. 12–13; p. 14; pp. 20–21; Siberian tiger, p. 23); **Photo New Zealand:** Alamy (cheetah, cover); Arco/R.Siegel (cheetah and cubs, bottom, p. 19); **Tranz/Corbis** (lion, tiger, cover; pp. 1–2; pp. 4–5; leopard, jaguar, pp. 6–7; cheetah and cubs, pp. 10–11; antelope, gazelle, p. 13; carrying prey, consuming prey, pp. 18–19; jaguar, leopard, p. 22)

All illustrations and other photographs © Weldon Owen Education Inc.

# CONTENTS

# INVESTIGATE CATS

Have you ever heard
a house cat **ROAR?**
No! House cats cannot roar.
Only big cats such as lions can roar.

But all cats are alike in
some ways. They are all
hunters, or **predators**.
Wild cats must hunt
and eat other animals
for food.

Wild big cats are at the top of their **food chain**. Five kinds of cats are in the big cat family. They hunt in special ways.

Look at the chart to compare big cats.

Cheetah

Leopard

Lion

| Leopard | Lion | Cheetah | Tiger | Jaguar |
|---|---|---|---|---|
| **Length:** about 7–9½ feet from head to tail | **Length:** about 8–10 feet from head to tail | **Length:** about 6–7 feet from head to tail | **Length:** most 8–10 feet from head to tail. Siberian 13 feet. | **Length:** about 5–8½ feet from head to tail |
| **Weight:** about 100–180 pounds | **Weight:** about 300–550 pounds | **Weight:** about 75–130 pounds | **Weight:** about 300–500 pounds. Siberian up to 660 pounds. | **Weight:** about 150–300 pounds |
| **Territory:** Africa, Asia | **Territory:** Africa, small area of India | **Territory:** parts of Africa | **Territory:** Asia | **Territory:** Central and South America |
| **Markings:** rings, spots | **Markings:** none, males have a mane | **Markings:** spots, tear marks | **Markings:** striped, with white belly | **Markings:** rings with spots inside |
| **Prey:** includes warthogs, hares, antelopes | **Prey:** includes zebras, antelopes, buffaloes | **Prey:** includes antelopes, hares, gazelles | **Prey:** includes deer, wild pigs, buffaloes | **Prey:** wild pigs, deer |
| **Special feature:** Some leopards have dark coats to better hide in the jungle. | **Special feature:** Lions live in groups called prides. Female lions hunt together. | **Special feature:** Cheetahs do not roar; they purr. Cheetahs use speed to hunt and survive. | **Special feature:** A striped coat helps a tiger hide as it hunts prey. Tigers are the only striped big cat. | **Special feature:** Jaguars are the only big cat that kills prey with a powerful bite to the back of the head. |

Jaguar

Tiger

# MAMA CHEETAH HUNTS

Mama cheetah lives in Africa. She is gentle and shy. She takes good care of her cubs.

Mama cheetah has a big **litter**.
She keeps her cubs clean.
She keeps them safe.
She teaches them how to hunt.

A big litter means lots of mouths to feed.

# DANGER!

Lions and hyenas are predators too. Sometimes they hunt cheetah cubs.

Lion

Hyena

11

Mama cheetah looks for **prey** almost every day. The lions stole her food yesterday. She and her cubs are hungry!

Cheetahs run faster than any other animal. But cheetahs catch only about half the animals they chase.

PREY

Antelope

Gazelle

13

Mama cheetah sees an antelope.
She **stalks** the animal.
She hides in the tall grass.
Her spots **camouflage** her well.
Mama cheetah moves slowly.
She does not want to be seen.

# SPOT THE DIFFERENCE!

Cheetahs have tear marks below their eyes. Jaguars have rings with small spots inside. Leopards have rings.

**Cheetah**

**Tear mark**

**Jaguar**

**Leopard**

15

Mama cheetah is very close
to her prey now. She bursts out
of the tall grass. She runs fast.

The antelope sees Mama cheetah.
It runs. It dodges to the right.
So does Mama. It dodges to the left.
Mama does too.

Then Mama cheetah leaps.

Mama cheetah knocks
down the antelope.
She bites its throat.
The chase is over
in less than 20 seconds.

She brings her prey to a safe place.

Mama cheetah
shares her food
with her cubs.

Mama cheetah and her cubs
are not hungry now.
They are sleepy after
their big meal.
It is time to clean up
and take a nap.

They all purr. It has been a good day.

## KING OF BEASTS

A lion's roar can be heard more than 5 miles away. The lion is called the "king of beasts."

## STRONGEST

Jaguars are the strongest big cats for their size. A jaguar can kill a cow that weighs more than itself.

## BEST CLIMBER

Leopards are the best climbers of all big cats. A leopard can climb as high as 50 feet up a tree with prey in its mouth.

# BIG CAT CHAMPIONS

Many big cats are champions! How do big cats compare?

## CHAMPIONS

**FASTEST**

A cheetah can run as fast as 70 miles per hour.

**BIGGEST**

The Siberian tiger is the largest of all the big cats. It is the only cat larger than a lion.

## MEASURE AND COMPARE

Claw

The paw is this wide.

The paw is this long.

Paw

0   1   2   3   4

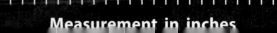

Measurement in inches

Tigers have the biggest
paws of all big cats.
This shows the real size
of a tiger's paw.

Measure the paw.
How wide is it?
How long is it?

Compare your
hand to the paw.
Which is WIDER?

Compare your
foot to the paw.
Which is LONGER?

Measure a claw.
How long is it?

**camouflage** – to hide or blend in with surroundings

**food chain** – a group of living things linked together because each one feeds on the one below it in the chain

**litter** – a group of baby animals, such as cubs, born at the same time to the same mother

**predator** – an animal that hunts and eats other animals

**prey** – an animal that is hunted and eaten by other animals

**stalk** – to hunt in a slow and quiet way

**Jaguar cubs**

There are not many big cats left in the wild. People have made wild land into cities and farms. Big cats are losing their homes. Now people are trying to save big cats. Find out more.

### Book

Gerrard, Hannah.
*Let's Talk Tigers*
(Brain Bank).
Scholastic Inc., 2006.

### Web Site

www.kids.nationalgeographic.com/Animals/
CreatureFeature/Cheetah

**Clouded leopard**